2 7 OCT 2015

2 5 AUG 2015

Driving my Tractor

Jan Dobbins & David Sim

D1331988

90712 000 002 289

Driving my tractor down a bumpy road,

And in my trailer, there's a heavy load.

There's a black-and-white cow
Going moo, moo, moo!
It's a very busy day.

Chug, chug,
Clank, clank, toot!

It's a very busy day.

Driving my tractor down a bumpy road,

And in my trailer, there's a heavy load.

There are two grey donkeys
Going bray, bray, bray!
It's a very busy day.

Chug, chug,
Clank, clank, toot!

It's a very busy day.

Driving my tractor down a bumpy road,

And in my trailer, there's a heavy load.

There are three pink pigs
Going oink, oink, oink!

It's a very
busy day.

Chug, chug,
Clank, clank, toot!
It's a very busy day.

Driving my tractor down a bumpy road,

And in my trailer, there's a heavy load.

There are four white lambs
Going mah, mah, mah!
It's a very busy day.

Driving my tractor down a bumpy road,

And in my trailer, there's a heavy load.

There are five brown chickens
Going cluck, cluck, cluck!
It's a very busy day.

Chug, chug,
Clank, clank, toot!

It's a very busy day.

Driving my tractor down a bumpy road,
The trailer hit a stone and it shook my load.

The animals fell out, and they ran away!

It's a very busy day.

Driving my tractor back home again,
Chugging along down the bumpy lane,

All the animals waiting for me!
Chug, chug, clank, clank, toot!

It's a very busy day.
PHEW!

Farmers have lots of different machines to help them with their work.

Trailers carry foodstuffs, animals and other equipment.

Tractors tow heavy equipment, such as trailers and ploughs.

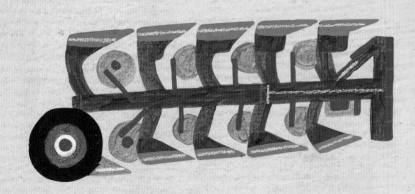

Ploughs turn the soil to make it ready for sowing seeds.

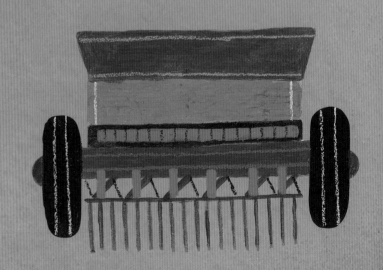

Seed drills plant seeds deep in the soil.

Combine harvesters cut wheat, oats and barley and separate the grain from the stems.

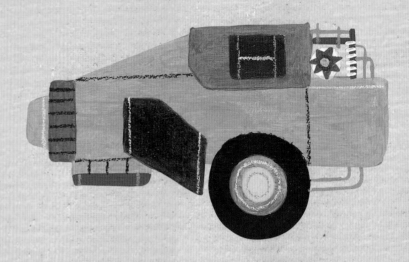

Balers gather harvested grain stems or mown grass and make them into bales of straw or hay.

Trucks transport smaller items than trailers and are designed to move easily across rough ground.

Milk trucks take milk from dairy farms to factories.

These are some of the crops that farmers grow.

Potatoes and sweet potatoes are sown in spring and are ready to be harvested when they have flowered.

Carrots are grown from seeds. They can be cultivated nearly all year round.

Sunflowers can be grow during the summer.

Beetroot is sown in spring and harvested from summer to autumn.

Onions and leeks are planted in spring, and are usually ready to eat by mid-summer.

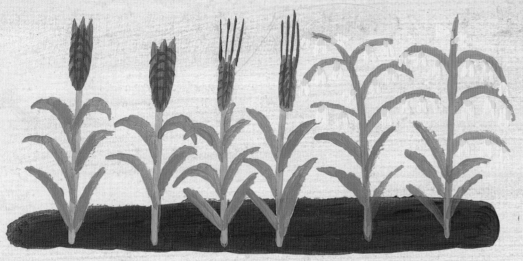

Wheat, barley and oats are cereal crops. They are usually sown in spring and harvested during late summer.

Marrow, squash and pumpkins are sown in late spring or early summer. They can be picked when quite young, or left to grow larger.

Sweet corn is a cereal crop. It is sown in spring.

Cabbages, cauliflowers, swedes and turnips are usually sown in spring and harvested in summer or autumn. Cabbages are also grown in winter.

Driving my Tractor